Mucky Medicine

Haydn Middleton

What's Up, Doc?

People have been around for thousands of years. And for thousands of years they've been getting ill. So doctors have always been very busy. But doctors haven't *always* had the same ideas about illness and medicine. In this book you'll find out about some of the weird things they used to think – and some of the seriously **MUCKY** things they used to do to their patients. If you're not feeling ill when you start reading this, you probably will be by the time you finish!

As you bash on through this book, write down and keep your answers to each **QUIZ** *question. (Remember, the answers are in the book!) OK? The doctor will see you now …*

MID-1300s

Poison from Another Planet?

All wiped out? You've got the Black Death!

PAGES 18 TO 21

1500–1700

Focus on Fluids

Stuffed with blood? Off to the barber!

PAGES 22 TO 27

1800s

Chop and Change

Need to lose a leg? Don't lose your life!

PAGES 28 TO 31

Spiteful Spirits

20,000 BC – 1000 BC

Ever heard anyone say, 'I need that like I need a hole in the head'? Well, thousands of years ago, men and women *did* have holes made in their heads – we've still got their skulls to prove it! Why did doctors suggest this form of treatment? We don't know for sure, because they left no written records. But modern experts think it was to let out 'evil spirits' who were causing pain and illness. The bit of skull that was removed was often kept afterwards – maybe as a charm to make sure the spirits stayed away!

FRaCTuRe FaCT

Did ancient doctors think evil spirits made your bones break and fracture too? Maybe. But they worked out a good way to mend them – making 'casts' out of clay and animal poo! Luckily, we have plaster casts today.

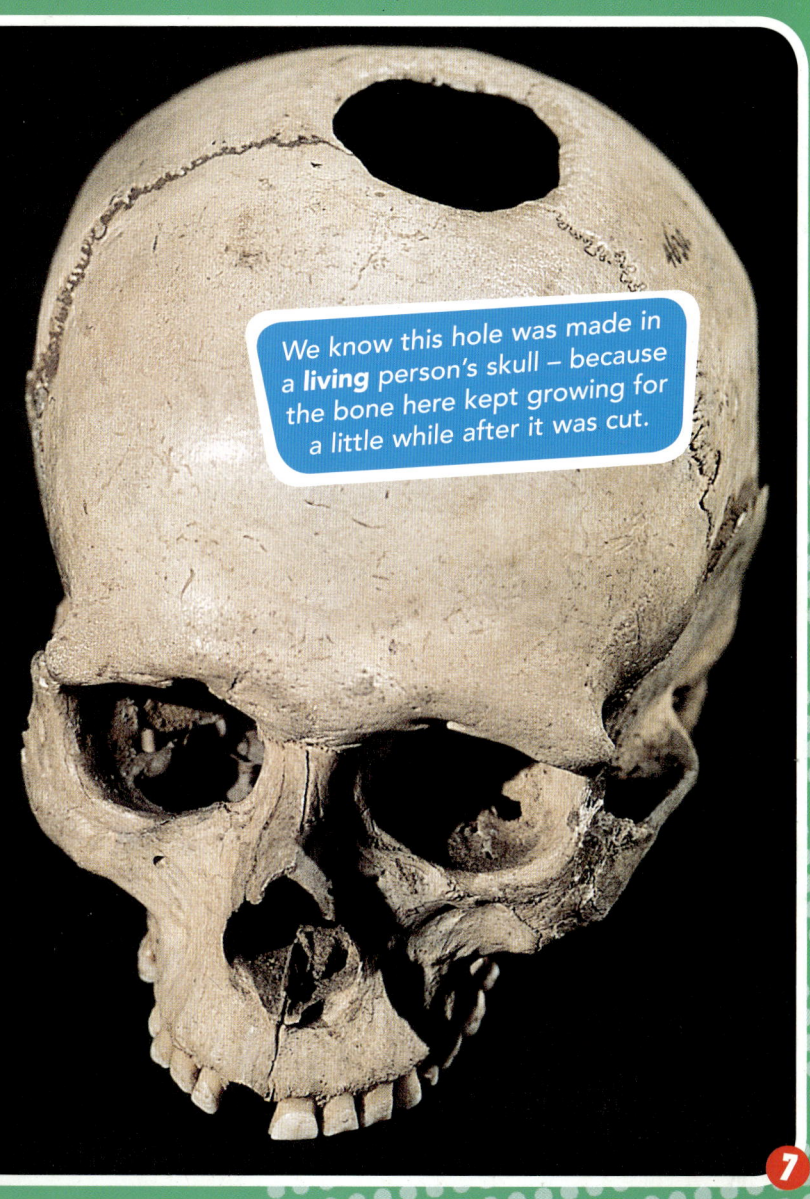

We know this hole was made in a **living** person's skull – because the bone here kept growing for a little while after it was cut.

The ancient Aborigines of Australia *definitely* believed evil spirits could get into your body and make you ill. They also thought if you were sick, your *own* spirit had been captured by an enemy! This enemy would have used a special 'pointing bone' to drag your spirit out. How could this 'illness' be treated? By trying to find the bone – with your spirit still attached to it!

The Aborigine doctor or 'medicine man' had a strange way of stopping an evil spirit from making you ill. First he sang and chanted until you were in a trance. Then he massaged the place where you were feeling sore or sick. Finally he ordered the spirit to come out of your body. When the naughty spirit obeyed, he captured it in a crystal!

The doctors of ancient Egypt also believed evil spirits made you sick. But they had different ways of dealing with them. They fed you with medicines made from herbs, minerals and bits of animals. They believed the medicine's taste or smell would drive the evil spirits away – but **only if** the doctors spoke exactly the right words too. If a doctor did *not* say the right words and you died, he could be executed!

Doctor, Doctor!

Doctor, Doctor! I feel awful. My ear is aching and my neck has gone all stiff!

Hmm. Feeling lousy – have a mousy! Rub mouse fat on the places where it hurts. If that doesn't work, swallow a whole mouse – but remember to take the skin off first!

QUIZ Ancient doctors made holes in people's

Pregnant women in ancient Egypt wore hippo charms, like this one, to frighten off evil spirits. The hippos in these charms were pregnant too!

✶✶✶✶✶ **while they were still alive!**

Getting in Balance

500 BC – 200 AD

According to some ancient Greek doctors, everyone had four important liquids inside them:

Blood
hot and wet
(giving you energy)

Phlegm (snot)
cold and wet
(helping you to cool down)

Yellow bile
hot and dry
(helping you to digest food)

Black bile
cold and dry
(bit mysterious, this one!)

If these liquids all stayed in the right balance, you had good health. If they got out of balance, you had to go and see the doctor!

FuNNY FaCT

The Greeks called the 4 liquids, the 4 'humours'. But they didn't always make you funny! If you usually had too much yellow bile inside you, you were likely to be a bad-tempered person; too much black bile and you tended to look on the dark side of things.

The ancient Greeks were very keen on the number 4. They thought the world was made up of 4 'elements' – air, fire, earth, and water. Like us, they also divided up the year into 4 seasons – spring, summer, autumn, and winter. In a pretty neat way, they linked up the 4 body liquids with the 4 elements *and* the 4 seasons …

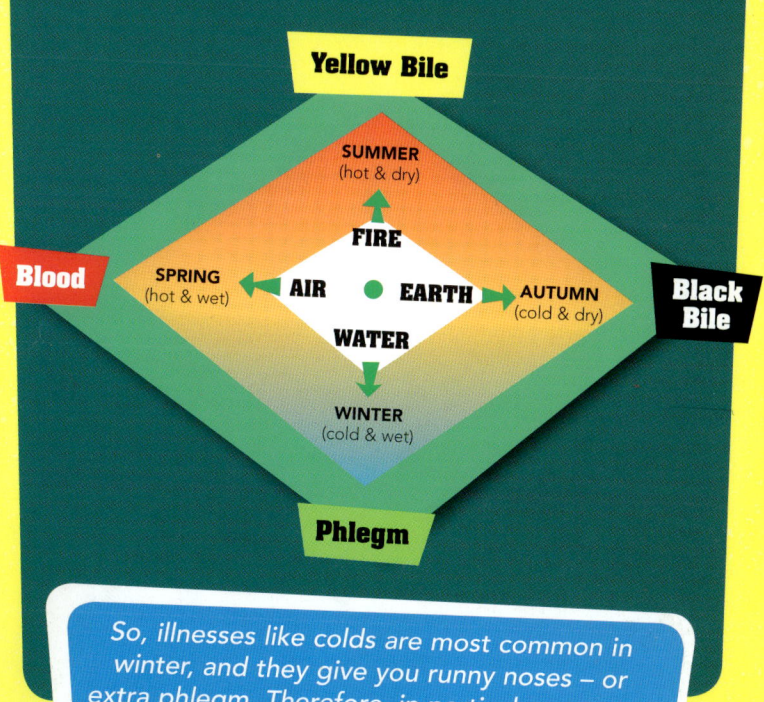

So, illnesses like colds are most common in winter, and they give you runny noses – or extra phlegm. Therefore, in particular seasons, you're more likely to get particular illnesses!

Doctor, Doctor!

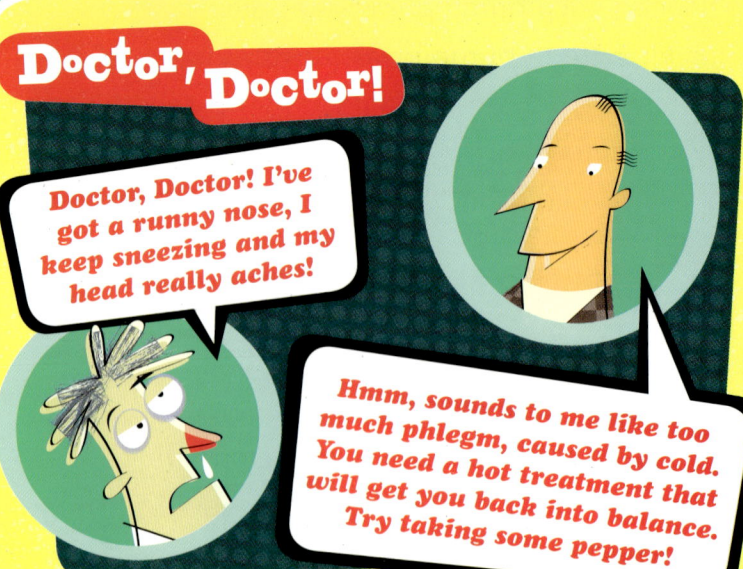

Doctor, Doctor! I've got a runny nose, I keep sneezing and my head really aches!

Hmm, sounds to me like too much phlegm, caused by cold. You need a hot treatment that will get you back into balance. Try taking some pepper!

The doctor who suggested pepper was called Galen. He worked in ancient Rome, treating injured gladiators. Gladiators were armed men who entertained huge crowds by fighting each other – sometimes to the death. Galen learned a lot about the human body from trying to heal their horrible wounds!

QUIZ Bile is a body liquid that comes in two

Galen wanted to chop up the bodies of dead gladiators. Then he could have found *exactly* how all the bits of the body fitted together and balanced each other. But it was against the law to mess around with dead people's bodies, so he had to make do with **animals!**

Where's my pig?

Er ... wouldn't you like to study a rat today instead?

colours: black and ✶✶✶✶✶✶.

Touch and Go!

Mid-1300s

Poison from Another Planet?

Some diseases keep you in bed for just a few days. The Black Death *killed* one European person out of every three. That's around **25 million people!**

Doctor, Doctor!

Doctor, Doctor! I'm DYING! Fever, headaches, vomiting, big black boils in my armpits! Everyone else in the village has got it too!

Hmm, this would be the Black Death. It's a poison in the air. Don't eat or drink too much – and don't have any hot baths. That will only open up your skin's pores and let more poisonous air in.

For almost 400 years after 1350, the Black Death kept breaking out. Even today we're not *exactly* sure what caused it. Doctors in the 1300s dreamed up all sorts of explanations – and treatments. Some believed the trouble started when the planets Saturn, Jupiter and Mars got too close together in space. No real cure for *that*!

Remember the guy in fancy dress on page 3? Well, why did medieval doctors wear these weird outfits? To keep them safe! The 'beak' was filled with sweet-smelling herbs, which they thought would protect them from the Black Death. They also wore hoods tied at the neck, long leather gowns and leather gloves, just to make sure the disease didn't spread to them.

CAUSES OF THE BLACK DEATH
What the Doctors Thought!

God was fed up with people sinning, so he sent the disease as a punishment.

Naughty people were poisoning the water in the wells.

Everyone's body liquids had got horribly out of balance.

Earthquakes had released poisonous fumes into the world.

20 QUIZ Body ✶✶✶✶✶✶✶ getting out of balance

So, doctors didn't really know WHAT to think. Many scientists today blame two little pests for the Black Death. The rat and the flea! Fleas were full of deadly bacteria and they travelled from Asia to Europe on rats! They bit the rats to suck their blood, infected them and killed them off. Then they started looking around for a fresh blood-supply ... **people!**

These people flogged themselves! Why? They wanted to show God how sorry they were for being sinful. They hoped it would stop them getting the Black Death.

FoWL FaCT

NO WAY!

This was one 'treatment' for Black Death boils: "Take a chicken and strip off feathers around its bottom. Then place bottom on one of the boils – to draw out poison."

was one explanation for the Black Death.

Focus on Fluids

1500 – 1700

In 1500, you didn't have to see the doctor to find out what was wrong with you. You just sent along a sample of your urine instead! The doctor took a good long look at it – checking how cloudy or clear it was, and exactly what colour it was. Then he used a chart like this to work out what was making you ill.

Once he'd identified your problem, the doctor came up with a suitable treatment. He might suggest medicines made from herbs or dead animal parts. Or he might reach for a *living* leech – that's a land worm with a sucker at each end. How did this mucky minibeast help the sick?

Turn over to find out!

FREAKY FACT
One mucky medicine was a lotion for a wound made by a sword. It had worms in it – and pig's brains. But you put it on the sword, not your wound – then magically you got better!

If your wee was black, you wouldn't need the doctor for long. Black meant you were going to die!

It sucked your blood!

Doctors put blood-sucking leeches on your skin to slurp off any extra 'bad blood' you might have. Then hey presto – your liquids would be back in balance! But if the doctor thought you needed to lose a *lot* of blood – three to four pints – he would send you to … the barber! As a sideline, some cutters of hair also cut into *you*. And since there were no hospitals like today, they even performed operations!

So what'll it be today, Sir?

Henry VIII haircut – 1 groat
Bloodletting – 5 groats
Leg removal – 10 groats

Before the 1600s, doctors thought your body kept making blood, using it up, then making more. Then they found it actually flowed round and round inside you, pumped by your heart. They realised this after chopping open *living* creatures – like frogs – and watching what went on under their skin. Bit by bit, doctors were getting *less* superstitious and *more* scientific about medicine. But they still had some pretty weird ideas about treatments …

Doctor, Doctor!

Doctor, Doctor! I'm in terrible trouble – I've been shot in the leg!

Hmm, that wound looks nasty. There's poison in the gunpowder so we must get rid of that first. Hold still while I pour some boiling hot oil on it! Ready?

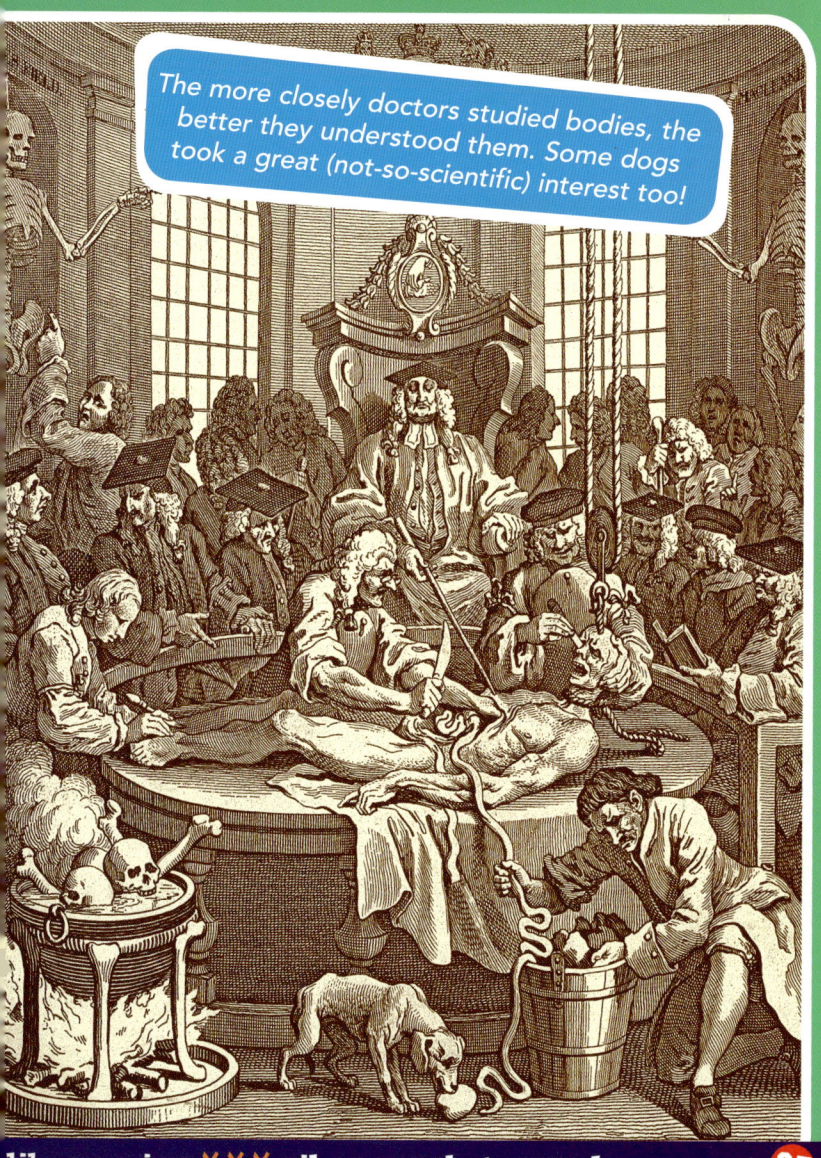

like pouring ✳✳✳ oil on gunshot wounds.

Chop and Change

1800s

When a bit of your body gave you just **too much** pain, there was only one solution – chop it off! But the pain caused by such an operation could be even worse – until a change took place in the mid-1800s …

Doctor, Doctor!

Doctor, Doctor! You said you'd have to chop off my bad leg. When will you start the operation?

I've done it already, my good man. It took me just 26 seconds!

How could you lose a leg without knowing it? By taking a whiff of 'ether' just before your operation – to relax your body. Another new chemical in the mid-1800s, 'chloroform', also put you in a deep, relaxing sleep. Until then, you just had to grin and bear it in the operating room. Think how much fun it must have been to have a bit of your skull removed (see page 7) without any painkillers first!

A doctor really did chop a man's leg off in 26 seconds! It was Robert Liston – a London doctor, in 1846. But Dr Liston could be too speedy sometimes. During one operation he also chopped off his assistant's fingers!

Operations were getting less *painful*, but until the late-1800s they were still incredibly *dangerous*. After the operations, patients kept dying of mysterious infections – until scientists spotted what was causing them: **germs** in the open wounds. It was time for the chopping doctors to clean up their act. So they swung into action with *disinfectants*.

FiLTHY FaCT

Doctors used to be seriously mucky! They re-used old bandages and didn't wash their hands before an operation. They even operated in clothes stained by previous patients' pus and blood – to prove how 'experienced' they were!

Trust me, I'm a doctor!

QUIZ Dr Liston used ✱✱✱✱✱ as a painkiller,

One of the first disinfectants was carbolic acid. It really stank – people had used it before to kill the nasty smell at sewage works! But by spraying it on the doctor's hands and knives (*and* on the patient) there was a far better chance of everyone coming out of the operation room alive!

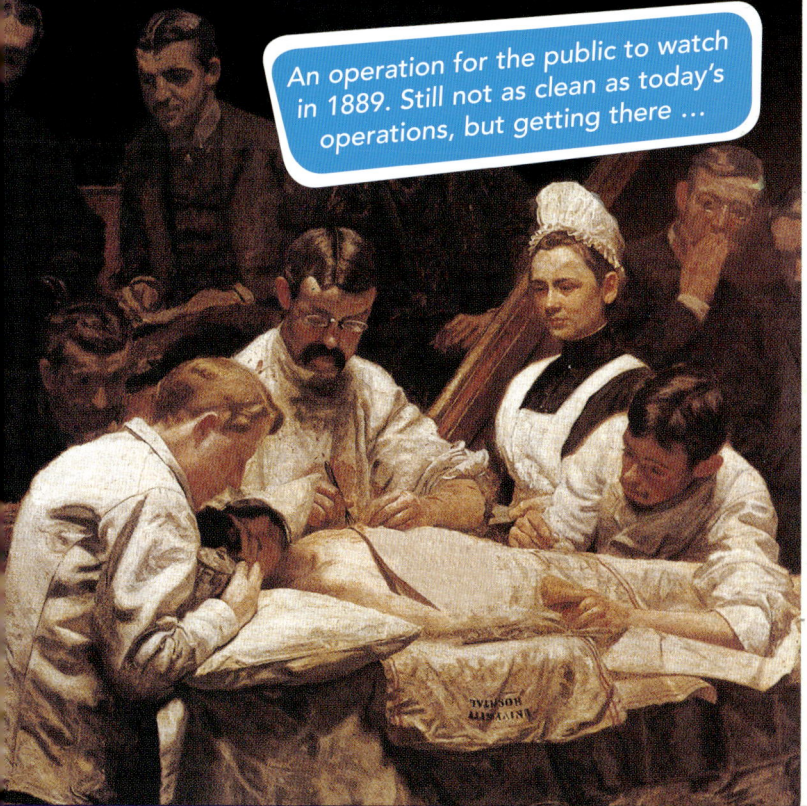

An operation for the public to watch in 1889. Still not as clean as today's operations, but getting there …